WALKING THE
CAMINO *of* LIFE

ASCENSION MENA

ISBN 978-1-0980-0201-5 (paperback)
ISBN 978-1-0980-0202-2 (digital)

Christian Faith Publishing, Inc.
832 Park Avenue
Meadville, PA 16335
www.christianfaithpublishing.com

Printed in the United States of America

EL CAMINO DE DIOS

I learned about El Camino de Santiago in 2012 when I saw the movie *The Way*, starring Martin Sheen and his son, Emilio Estevez. I was touched by the spirituality of the events in the movie, and it sparked an interest that culminated into a pivotal phase of my faith life. At that time, I was very deep into my faith journey, and I was discovering a very powerful spirituality that was transforming me into a fisher of men. It was another ingredient that I needed to make me whole. Peregrinos or Pilgrims have been walking this Pilgrimage Walk for centuries in Europe, mainly in northern Spain. It officially starts at St. Jean Pied du Port in France, goes over the Pyrenees Mountains to Roncesvalles, Spain, and continues across northern Spain to Santiago de Compostela, circa 480 miles. Since then, I have walked the Camino a total of seven times. I have been on the Camino by myself twice, with my brothers Roberto Truax, Johnny Casarez, Jorge Valenzuela, Jesse Marrufo, and Elias Torrez on my other Walks. My wife, Mimi, my daughter, Gaby, and my son, Angel Edward, have also completed the Walk with me. The Walk allows you to see time in a whole new dimension, distance as a variable of how you see time and self-awareness of feelings that you hold deep in your being.

On the Camino with my Acts Brother and neighbor Elias

On the Camino with my brothers, Roberto and Jorge

Jesse, Roberto, Johnny. Great company on the Camino

With my family on the Camino

Mimi, Angel, Gaby, and Me on the outskirts of Santiago de Compostela

The Apostle James (Santiago) evangelized in northern Spain and his remains are preserved at the Cathedral of Santiago de Compostela. There are two routes in northeastern Spain that begin in the Spanish-French Border and several others that originate in Portugal and western Spain. All Caminos lead to Santiago de Compostela, although some Peregrinos continue to Finisterre (The end of the world). Finisterre is where the road ends on KM 0.

Gaby and Angel in Finisterre

The Romans believed that it was the end of the world, therefore the name Finisterre. Many Pilgrims burn their clothes at Finisterre or leave clothes as mementos of their Walk. I mused for a period of weeks and decided that I could do the Walk. I began training every day for 3–4 months, walking 3–5 miles daily, walking everywhere, taking some 15 miles walks on the weekends and doing research online. I read about the Albergues (hostels), trains, buses, food, terrain, weather, costs, airlines, food, etc. I had no idea what I was doing until I got there and realized that no amount of reading or plans had prepared me for the journey of my life. As a farmworker child living in rural New Mexico and being a voracious reader, I promised myself that I would travel the world and up to that point in my life I had traveled throughout Central and South America, Europe, and Asia. Presently (April 2018) I am on my seventh Camino and am resting from the Walk in Santiago.

Growing up in rural New Mexico, I looked forward to going to the school library and reading all the books that were there. I recall taking home at least 3–4 books daily, everything from biology, chemistry, scientist autobiographies, nature books, travel books, and anything I could get my hands on. Did all these books influence my careers in biology/chemistry, research, and medicine? I can say that this habit, that came out of nowhere, helped shape my professional life. I have brought friends and family on the five previous Walks, but this Walk I took alone. I felt a yearning to be by myself, and I envisioned Him waiting for me to join Him on this Walk. I see Him walking next to me in a frantic pace with a broad smile and kind eyes. I can't touch any of his substance except what I see. I believe that He gives me knowledge when it is time or when I am ready. To focus on Him throughout the entire Walk, to talk to Him, to feel His smile, to hear His voice, to teach me more, to learn more from Him—what gifts! I could hardly wait to start my Walk. I felt that I was walking in the desert by myself and I longed to walk with Him as soon as I could. Up to that time, I had witnessed events that could only have been of divine origin. My world was not simple at all. It was like a tapestry that was being woven in front of me, and I knew that there was more to come. I had many domestic and business

On top of the Pyrenees

commitments, but I was going to keep my promise to Walk with Him. You see, the Lord gives you many gifts along the Way and your heart and spirit are elevated to an unknown universe. If you "feel" the Camino, you will experience this feeling. On my third Walk, while at the Cruz de Hierro, I received the gift of more Life. My father had passed away at age 66, and I was scared that I would not fare any better. I don't smoke, drink, or have any bad habits that would be detrimental to my health. I practiced Emergency Room medicine over 20 years, and death was no stranger to me. However, I lived through the physician nightmare of attending my own father when he became unresponsive at home. My mother Valeria called me and told me my father was disoriented when I had finished my ER shift and I rushed to their home. I was not able to revive him at home or en route to the hospital in the ambulance. My mother joined me in the hospital after he passed away, and my sorrows became even greater because of the pain she was feeling. She told me that my father was the only man she had ever loved, and she held his hand and cried until it was time to leave. This is a physician's nightmare. I wish this on no one, and deep inside, I harbored a fear that I never shared with anyone. Although I have had a relatively healthy lifestyle, I know

My Family on the Camino

the role that genetics plays in life. I lived with the fear that my life would be cut short like my father for years to come, and I opened my heart to my Lord at the Iron Cross after so many years of fear.

*Sometimes, you run into hometown friends on the Camino.
Here with our friend Mike from El Paso!*

We had spent the night in Astorga on the way to the Cruz de Hierro when I heard Him say to me that He was going to take me home in six years, but that since I was faithful and had kept my word to go back, He was giving me six more years and twenty more!

Physically exhausted at times…spiritually exalted always

My brother Roberto at the Cruz;
Mimi and Angel at an Albergue

I felt as if my chest was on fire, and I ran down the Cruz about a mile when I remembered that I had left my two friends back at the Cruz! I went back to get them and we continued our Walk, but my legs were lighter, my smile was hard to contain, and if I had had wings, I would have flown to Santiago.

Miracles along the Way

Every Walk has been different for me. On my first Walk, I carried my prayers for the daughter of a friend who was suffering from myasthenia gravis and had been told that her condition would deteriorate rapidly and that she would probably be bed and wheelchair bound. I prayed to Santiago to intercede for Marti in such a way that I was exhausted beyond belief when I finished my prayer for Marti. On my second Walk, I checked in on my email account and was given the news by Marti's dad (Leroy) that the physicians at the Mayo Clinic could find no evidence or markers of the disease! The physicians could not explain it and said that she was "in remission," but Marti and her family knew better. The Mayo Clinic is the premier clinic in the United States and I have referred many patients with hard to treat illnesses. The last I heard, Marti was running marathons in Iowa. A Miracle granted.

On the second Walk, I prayed with my entire heart and soul for Santiago to intercede on behalf of a friend's brother who was suffering from multiple myeloma and was not expected to live long. He was in and out of the hospital frequently and he was losing hope. He was going to undergo some new treatments, and I could see the sadness in his children's eyes. That was six years ago, and Rudy has recovered. He looks strong, is back at work, and is a new creation. Another Miracle.

Every year that I take prayers to Santiago, it feels like I am drinking fresh water in the middle of the desert. I am exhausted, but my thirst is quenched. I'll spend 3–4 hours in prayers that I take to Santiago and am spiritually and physically exhausted. One year, I took pictures of all the prayers with my iPhone and that was the year that the airlines lost my backpack, but I had the prayers on my phone! I had to buy the entire travel gear on the first day, but I suffered because of the lack of hiking socks, hiking boots, pants, other usual supplies needed daily. I finally recouped my backpack from the airlines 4 months later, but I learned humility on that Walk. Your best laid plans may go totally wrong. Faith is needed in abundance. Another lesson learned.

If you go on the Camino and do not feel the urgency to go back, whether you do or not, then you learned very little or nothing at all. I have read that you must share whatever the Camino teaches you or it will be lost. On this last Walk, I read along the way that you should not hurry along the Camino because the only one you are going to meet is you. As soon as your blisters and sprains heal, you want to go back. After each Walk and after I heal, my heart and soul are already preparing for the next Walk.

As I said before, I have been on the Camino seven times. I walked by myself on the first Camino, brought several friends and family on the others, but this one was mine alone. I have tended to Peregrinos with injuries, blisters, wound infections, and one Peregrino who was having chest pain. On this Walk, it was I who was hurting. I was severely wounded in my soul and needed to feel my Father's love and maybe, if possible, begin to heal or to understand the pain inside of me. I was feeling betrayed, I was trying to understand what had just happened and was trying to give it up to my Lord so he could explain my feelings. I couldn't explain this pain to other parishioners and friends, but my wife Mimi and my youngest children, Gaby and Angel, could feel my pain and despair. They could feel my pain, but they too knew that I had to go back to the Walk to soothe my wounds that were very profound.

The Camino is a Walk with God. It is a physical walk that seems to never end, and when it does is accompanied by aches, pains, blisters, self-doubt, heart break off-on throughout the Walk, and counterbalanced with hope, faith, assurance, comfort, love. If you do not experience these feelings and thoughts, then you have to Walk again. The goal (meta) is not Santiago de Compostela, it is the road, it is the steams, mountains, the smiles of the people, it is the constant reminder that we all have a Camino, a Way that is always there. All we have to do is walk it. Every one of my Walks seems to have had a purpose that I was not aware of.

Prayer at the Cruz de Hierro

My Walk began long before I ever knew it. It had taken me all the way from the fields in New Mexico to medical school at Michigan State University, a very improbable event, given the times of turmoil in the US from the 50s to the 60s. Those were times of horrible discrimination, dehumanization, and a war across the world that was simmering. History seems to be repeating itself. My country is presently in one of the longest wars in history in Iraq and Afghanistan. We are at odds with so many countries that it seems that a darkness and a sadness has fallen over the land. There is boastful talk of a nuclear war when we should be talking of world peace through dialogue and following the tenets of our faith. We apparently did not learn our lesson from the *Art of War* (Sun Tzu).

God was merciful with me since I was born and He continues to care for me. I hear Him in the night and I can see Him telling me to focus on Him on my Walks. I miss my personal time with Him between Walks and my body feels the longing to be at His side. My body is taking longer to heal, but my faith and soul are stronger. I have walked over 14,000 miles over the last 9 years. That in itself is a blessing to my health.

*At the End
of the World*

    As I mentioned, my family and I grew up in the fields of New Mexico. We moved to El Paso, Texas, where I graduated from High School and UT-El Paso, before moving on to Michigan State where I became a physician. My father was in the Bracero Program and he sent for us when I was 5 years old. We worked in the fields until I was 15 years old when we moved to El Paso, Texas. I graduated from high school, attended college and graduate school, and went off to medical school. After my training, I returned to El Paso where I have practiced medicine (34 years). I was blessed with an instinct for business and set up several successful businesses, besides my medical practice. I was becoming a typical physician, well off, into material things, travel, golf. I was good friends with an old high school friend who invited me to men's spiritual retreat. He had introduced me to Monsignor Frank Smith who was to be my mentor on a journey that would define my spirituality.

I attended a men's ACTS retreat, and I really didn't think much of it until a week later when I began seeing things differently. ACTS is a spiritually retreat that originated in Selma, Texas, and has spread throughout the US and other parts of the world. I walked around in a daze and at night (usually 3 a.m.) I began to envision buildings, a chapel, a desert, and I had no idea what was going on. When I look back at that time in my life, I remember talking to my wife, and she suggested that I pray when I received those visions. I prayed at that time numerous times and I received the vision to build a spiritual retreat center in late 2006. The Lord led me to a place out in the desert in far east El Paso. I discussed it with Monsignor Smith, and we decided that it was not practical and so I continued my search. Not that easy.

Chuy Loya and Epi Parra there after I began building

We had had a massive rainstorm in August of that year and I was delighted to be able to shore up my son's house to protect him from the floods. I had just bought a tractor for no apparent reason and was able to put it to use immediately. Thankfully, my son's house was saved and I was able to help some of his neighbors, as well. When I think back to this time, it is just a small piece of the tapestry that was being woven. That tractor would be instrumental in building a miracle in the desert. I eventually found the right place and I began construction by myself. I began clearing the 10-acre parcel with a caterpillar tractor and announced to the ACTS men's group that I was starting the project. I used to look for visitors every day, but no one came for 30–40 days. It was then that I was adopted by a pregnant female pitbull (Baby) who became my companion for several years, along with her son, Carlos. They are no longer with me, but they were my angels when I was by myself. Certainly, this was not by chance. Slowly, the Lord sent some other ACTS brothers one by one: Pablo Rojo, Jake Olivas, Epi Parra, Jesus Carrasco, David Sanchez, George Gomez, Raul Bencomo, Fr. Charles, Elias Torrez, Johnny Casarez, Arturo Mena, Louie Gonzalez, Leroy Pickens, Hector Clemente, Jack Johnston, Rick Barnett, John Cataldi, Art Saenz, Lawrence Stewart and others started to see my vision. Some would stay for a little while and others would stay longer. The Retreat Center was a place for healing and many would leave when they had healed. In less than a year, we had built 44 individual bedrooms, a large conference center/dining room-cafeteria, a large chapel, and 3 other large buildings. We built the Retreat Center from the ground up; plumbing, electrical, cement, adobe, roofing, etc. A Miracle.

A community coming together

Angel helping erect the Dome

Always by my side

Nothing is ever easy. There is no path of least resistance when it is that important. Discernment may reveal that which you want to be done, that which can be done, and whether you can build it. Monsignor Smith was there to guide me on the initial part of the vision. I once read along the Camino a Monk's prayer that asks for strength from God at the beginning of each chore because the beginning is where one is the weakest. God gave me strength at this time that would carry me to initiate the sacred task and make me strong for the attacks that were to come, and they came fast and furious.

I remember that during my first year of medical school, I received a call from my friend Oscar who was dying of cancer. I had known Oscar since the eighth grade, and we became inseparable in college and graduate school at UTEP. I was in first year of medical school at Michigan State University when Oscar called me one night to say goodbye to me and he told me that he would be dying soon and wished me well. I told him that I would fly home as soon as I finished with my exams that week and to wait for me. Oscar died that week, and I was not able to see him before he passed. I really had to work hard at concentrating on my exams with a broken heart. Oscar was as close to being my brother as you can get. Oscar is buried close to my parents, and I visit him when I visit my parents at the cemetery. I miss my friend all the time.

When I broke ground at the site of the future retreat center, I faced a tempest that tested me, my faith, my family, and my heart.

In January 2007, my wife and I were invited to my friend Jorge's fiftieth birthday party and my wife Mimi noticed that all her dresses were too tight and didn't fit her right. After trying to dismiss it jokingly as a sign to go on a weight loss diet, I still had a premonition that this was not normal. The physician in me suspected something horrible and horrible it was. My wife was diagnosed with ovarian cancer the following week, had surgery by the end of January, and chemotherapy followed the next 2 months. My entire family came together, and by late April, my wife was helping me plant some trees at the retreat center. She had no hair, was very pale, tired, but she could light up the night sky with her smile. I recall seeing a man who had obviously been sick with cancer on the Camino. He was close to

Santiago de Compostela and was leaning against the wall, smiling. He looked as if he had just reached the top of Mt. Everest. He was radiating power from his entire body. I'll never forget his smile and his eyes. My wife was like that, and she is still with the Spirit. I could see God in their eyes.

Hope and Faith carried us during those 12 years.
My family's love kept me strong throughout.

My ACTS brothers helping out on a weekend

Every day I would tend to my wife, would take her to the office for a few hours, and then my sister or brother would take her home to rest. My sister-in-law and mother-in-law would alternate taking her for chemotherapy treatment and taking her home, helping with my two young kids at school, as well. I would return late from work and would tend to my two younger kids. Not too long ago, I mentioned to my wife that I would cry throughout the day during that time. She had no idea how hard her illness was on the entire family. But we never thought of stopping. We were to keep this frantic pace up until our first retreat in May 2007, only 7 months after I started the project! And we built most of the buildings with adobe. I became an expert on adobe, making and setting over 100,000 adobes over a 7-month period with other volunteers from the local ACTS groups that were becoming a force in the local Catholic community.

We held our first Men's ACTS retreat in May 2007, and I finally understood the urgency of holding this retreat when the center was still being built. As a physician, I always kept an eye on anyone who may have been sick, and I tried to greet all the groups when they arrived for their retreat. I noticed an ACTS retreatant on the first retreat in May 2007 who appeared to have kidney failure. On the last day of the retreat, I remember him smiling and interacting with his new brothers in faith. Men would arrive to the retreats frowning and apprehensive and would leave the Retreat Center as new creations, as new men. I learned that he had passed away 3 weeks later and that he had told friends and family that he was at peace with God. This was the reason that I worked so hard. Otro milagro.

Over the next 11 years, we were to host 250 retreats, bringing over 14,000 souls to retreat. We were to build 6 more buildings, renovate both homes on site over the next 11 years, but another storm was brewing all along.

I have always been a loner and would enjoy working by myself on the weekends where I would also plan and organize for the following week. It was during a Saturday morning that I had experienced an evil presence around me. I was laying adobe bricks on the floor of the Agape room when I felt a dark presence all around me. I could sense the power in the dark presence and an anger and rage in the presence as it surrounded me. I had never experienced such an ominous power, and for the first time in my life, I felt a sense of impending doom. I fell to my knees and began praying, feeling strong and vulnerable at the same time. I felt scared to the core, but I had faith that I possessed a greater power through prayer. I sensed that the darkness wanted to destroy me but could not get close to me. It seemed like those 10–15 minutes of fear were hours until the darkness left the room and I felt exhausted and relieved.

*Jesus Carrasco painted
the beautiful murals
and brought happiness
to Holy Trinity
Retreat Center*

I felt that two forces were fighting for my soul that Saturday morning. For every evil force, there has always been a force of goodness. That day I felt vulnerable like never before and trusted God to protect me, and He did. I have always looked for the darkness, have not seen it, but I know that it is always there. The Camino is not always straight, it is crooked, jagged, smooth at times, slippery at times and full of turns, with occasional easy paths. A friend of mine, Louie, has always said that we are also like the Camino, broken at times, crooked at times and lost at times. Our task is to always get back on the Camino, broken or hurt at times. It is when we deviate too much from our Way that we get lost and may never find our way back to the Camino. If we strive hard, we can see the yellow arrows pointing the way, not realizing that the arrow was there all along.

Arturo, Jake, Gaby, Angel, and Ruben

Forgiveness

I met Father Charlie at the beginning of 2006 and still see him once in a while. He has moved to Minnesota, Indiana, other places I don't know about and now he is in New Mexico. He shows up in El Paso for many Tigua Tribe festivities since he has a strong tie to the community here. He brought the Tigua Tribe closer to the El Paso Diocese, specifically Our Lady of Mt. Carmel Church. Father Charlie, like Monsignor Smith, would have an impact on my life for the next 12 years, if not forever.

It all started when I was building the Retreat Center. We built everything from the bottom up. We not only built the buildings, we built the sewer system, plumbing, electrical, and laid all the cement to the entire place. Most of the Center was built with adobe brick, which we made and set. The Retreat Center is located in Far East El Paso and is basically built on sand. We had to place base dirt and screening rock before we built on 10 acres. It was a huge undertaking.

We started having retreats even before we had solved all the problems of building an entire center, and of course, things would not always work or break down. It was during that time that I came across a fellow parishioner who would criticize the Retreat Center when

The Kiva was was built on-site, piece by piece. It became the Divine Mercy Chapel, all in less than 4 months. A Miracle in itself.

something would go wrong. The problem was that he would exaggerate every incident and I would get calls from the community about these so-called incidences. The problem I had is that I would see him in mass and he would greet me like I was his best friend. I talked to Father Charlie about this anger that was building up inside of me. Did this man have any idea of what I was doing and that my wife was ill? How could he criticize me? What right did he have to pass judgment on me? I struggled with this issue, and when I discussed this with Father Charlie, he told me that my anger was normal, but that I had to reach deep inside me, in the deepest part of me, and forgive this man. I told Father Charlie that I would forgive him. Father Charlie then told me that it was just not that easy to do and that I had to pray and meditate about the offense that was hurting me. I asked him how long would it take and he told me that I would know when it happened. Only God and I would know. This blessed event happened almost 2 months later when the anger disappeared, and I felt like a heavy burden had disappeared. The next time I saw this man, he appeared sad, but I did not feel any anger or rancor against him. He stopped coming to mass, and I wondered what had ever happened to him. I later learned that he was in trouble and Father Charlie asked me to pray for him. This was my first real lesson in Forgiveness. In all of this pain, there was redemption and forgiveness. Father Charlie was to reveal another important truth to me later when I let the Retreat Center go.

I would drive 25 miles to the Retreat Center every day for almost 8 months. One day I was driving to the Center when I felt a strange urge to a turn off the road into the desert. I felt something telling me to get off my truck and to walk toward some sand dunes. I got there, expecting to see someone or something else in need. I looked around and kept on walking around the area. I must have walked a half mile looking for something or someone in need. I was truly expecting to see someone or something, but I saw nothing. I started walking back to my truck and I was asking God why He had led me there if there was nothing to see or save. I was a physician and was used to helping others in need. Then I heard God telling me that He just wanted to make sure that I was listening to him. Nothing more. I was humbled by this reality and regained my focus, went to my truck, and went to work. I reminded myself that I had to remember to listen. I talked to God every day and began to listen more. The more I listened, the more I understood the power of the Retreat Center. The Retreat Center is truly a holy place with a power to grant favors to the faithful and to exact horrible retribution to those who blasphemed against it. I know of many tragedies that people who blasphemed suffered. I cannot and would not attempt to comprehend this. This was far from my spiritual level of understanding because I am just a man. I am witness to the power of God

Adobe is incredibly strong and is very durable, as long as it doesn't get wet or it will crumble. You have to cover the adobe with stucco and paint to protect it. One Saturday, I was working by myself and had covered the adobes that were drying outside. The large chapel, we call it a KIVA, was partially built but not covered. I looked to the East and saw a huge storm approaching fast. The sky became dark, and you could see lightning and a cloud of dust that was kicking up ahead of the rain storm, a harbinger of a strong rainstorm. I fought the best way I knew: I began praying that the storm go to the sides and not touch the Center. I was by myself and knew that there was no way that I could drape the tarps to protect the unfinished walls in the KIVA. When I opened my eyes, I saw that the storms had moved west. It was still cloudy, but the only place where the sun was shining was over the retreat center. The Retreat Center took on this golden reddish color, with no rain. I hurried and covered the KIVA with the large tarps, and after the tarps were secured, I thanked God and the rain began.

The Kiva today

It was during the week, sometime in March 2007, when we were finishing up a 6000 sq foot building that we were putting the metal sheets on the roof. The ceiling on the building is 35 ft at its apex of a high pitch roof. It was during the afternoon when we saw a storm approaching from the south. I became very anxious and was worried that we had not secured the metal sheets on the roof and that the metal sheets would be blown off, all of us included. Epi, my assistant, asked me to pray that the storm stop. The storm had come out of nowhere and it was one of the worst storms I had seen. The wind speed was well over 50 mph, accompanied by dust. After my prayers, the whole world seems to have stopped. The trees had stopped moving and even the birds were confused as to what was happening. Nothing was moving. The only place where the sun was shining was around us. We quickly ran back up to the roof and finished securing the metal sheets and finished. I had asked God to give us the opportunity to finish the roof because we would fall behind if the storm was allowed to hit us. I asked for His help because I had done everything he had asked me to do and only He could stop the rain. After we finished securing the roof, the rain and the wind began, but we had secured the roof and all was well. God's power is immense. Only He can stop the rain.

The soil in far east El Paso is mainly sand. In order to make a good adobe brick, you need soil that contains at least 60 percent clay. Since all we had was sand, I found a trucker who would bring me 40 tons of clay on each trip. I would mix the clay mix with straw, some screening rock, and we were producing up to 850 bricks per day. I would produce 2000 bricks initially to begin a project and then continue producing them daily until we finished each building. There is an abundance of clay in the lower valley and I lost track of how many truckloads we brought in. This also included screening rock for the mix and used as base throughout the Center. The adobe bricks weighed 22 lbs and it was hard work, especially hard on your back and arms. We used a hydraulic machine to compress the bricks and they could be set almost immediately. I would prepare the soil on the weekends with the help of my daughter, Gaby, and son, Angel. My wife, if she felt well, would come to the Center and help in other tasks.

Since I became a physician, I was always involved in multiple projects: ambulance companies, clinics, medical supplies, emergency rooms. I became focused when I started the Retreat Center and many things were placed on hold. My wife's illness, the challenge of funding the place by myself and hiring the right people demanded a lot of focus and planning. I felt that I had eye blinders on in order to focus all my energy on the project. I sought no funding or patronage from anyone. We continued donating to the Catholic Diocese education fund, Excellence fund and other charities in the area, besides the ACTS Missions out of San Antonio, Texas. We donated the gymnasium floor to Cathedral High School and helped with the renovation of their locker room. We did not shy away from donating to the community.

People feel the Peace at Holy Trinity Retreat Center

Before the project on the Retreat Center began, I had been buying and renovating apartment buildings as a retirement project. Prior to the collapse of housing market in 2008, I had sold all our properties and used those funds to build the Retreat Center. The housing market collapsed several months later, but I had secured funding for the project. A parishioner wrote me a check for 250 dollars as a donation, and I kept it in my wallet for 10 years until it disintegrated in my wallet. The trust my friend put in me was worth more to me than any other amount anyone could have given me.

So my life continued, thankfully my wife recovered, my two children moved on to college, and I continue my Walk with God on this Camino de Santiago, and I intend to continue on this yearly Walk until only one thing stops me. I look forward to embracing God at the end of my life on this earth and plan to listen to Him forever.

Jesse Marrufo at St. Jean Pied du Port.
The Beginning of the Camino

2017 was a challenging year for me. The ACTS movement began to lose steam, and I was not getting the support of my community/parishes. Retreats that had been scheduled a year in advance were being canceled routinely, some parishes canceling retreats altogether. My faith was severely tested that year, and I started to think of alternatives to keeping the Retreat Center. I entertained several offers, but I was skeptical that there would be no more retreats, which is the reason that I built it. I started researching alternatives but reached the ultimate conclusion that I could not afford to keep the Retreat Center because of the lack of support from my faith community and I knew that I had to decide quickly.

I met with the Diocese representatives, and we discussed selling the Retreat Center. We met at least three more times before we came to an agreement. The agreement was very unfair to me, but I knew that I did not need to profit from this project that was bathed in Holiness. The Diocese was very pleased that I offered it at such a low price and we agreed to it. I couldn't understand how the project had fallen apart, but I could not see it going to some other group or religion. My faith had to be stronger to let it go. I felt as if I was losing something so precious and priceless that I felt that I couldn't breathe for the rest of the day. I was donating 80 percent of the Center to the Diocese, but the alternative would be to close it or sell it to someone else and I could not live with myself. The decision was easy to make at the end, but I felt wounded. I had no problem giving it up, it just hurt that I was giving it up for reasons that I was not sure of. I have never done well with uncertainty. Twelve years of my life, my wife surviving her illness, all the friends that I came to know, and seeing the fruits of hard work were disappearing in front of my eyes. I had to testify that it was Miracle! This was not just some property that was being passed along. It was special. I sustained multiple injuries: lacerations, broken bones, neck injury, etc. Literally, sweat and tears. My children were with me when they were not in school and I never tired of showing visitors and friends the entire facility.

It was the place where many retreatants found their way. It was a place where people felt peace, where many had been saved. It was during this time that I knew that I needed to go on my Walk with Him. I imagined Him waiting for me on the Camino like before.

A friend of mine recently lost his son and his grandson and was in so much pain. I told him that his son and grandson were a blessing from God and that he had been a blessing for them as well. I told him that he should let God hold him in His arms just as he used to hold his son and grandson. I needed God to hold me closer because I was hurting. I left to my Walk and walked the last segment from OCebreiro to Santiago de Compostela.

I felt angry, distraught, confused, and wanted to listen to His voice. I wanted peace in my soul and wanted to lessen the pain. Had I stopped listening? Why did my faith community abandon me? Why did ACTS groups cancel retreats? What had I done wrong? Why did I feel that the Retreat Center was not appreciated as a Miracle and not just a transaction? Didn't anyone understand the Miracle of the retreat center and the miracles that I had witnessed? I walked the Camino carrying a cross that was very heavy, and I regained a sense of self again when I reached Santiago. I met people along the Camino looking for their own answers, looking for meaning to their life, seeing people with the same longing in their life, sharing their joy with others and blessing others along the way. I met a Peregrino from Oregon who asked me what I was doing on the Camino. We talked for a long time and I told him that the reason I came to the Walk was to give thanks to the Lord for my life, my family, my vocation, and for choosing me to minister to others. The sum total was a thanksgiving. He told me that he had been on the Camino for three weeks looking for answers. He said that he realized that he had been cruel to his ex-wife and that he could hardly wait to go back home and ask for her forgiveness. He told me that he knew it would not be easy and would pray for her forgiveness and maybe, just maybe she would take him back. He thanked me and I remember seeing him leave the albergue in the morning as a true Peregrino who knew where he was going.

I have not gone back to the Retreat Center since I passed it to the Diocese, and I have heard that retreats are being held again. I drove by the Retreat Center several weeks because I felt that my trees were calling me. We had over 80 pines and I loved those trees. I drove by and I could almost hear the Retreat Center telling me that everything was fine and that it was letting me go. I felt the Retreat Center had forgiven me for letting it go. It was one of the most painful moments in my life. Only God will tell me when I am cured of any doubts, of any pain, of any guilt. Only God will tell me when I can forgive myself and others.

I serve as Medical Director for the Ysleta del Sur Tigua Tribe emergency response/fire department, and I was at a ceremony called La Salida. The Diocesan priests were there and a Mass was being held prior to the ceremony. I looked around and saw Father Charlie. I went to greet him and he told me he had heard that I had sold the Retreat Center to the Diocese. I told him that that really wasn't the case and that I felt somewhat conflicted about the Retreat Center. He looked at me, smiled and said, "Sometimes that's the way things happen in order for greater things to happen." More miracles no doubt.

High school friends Ruben and David contributed their talent and ideas

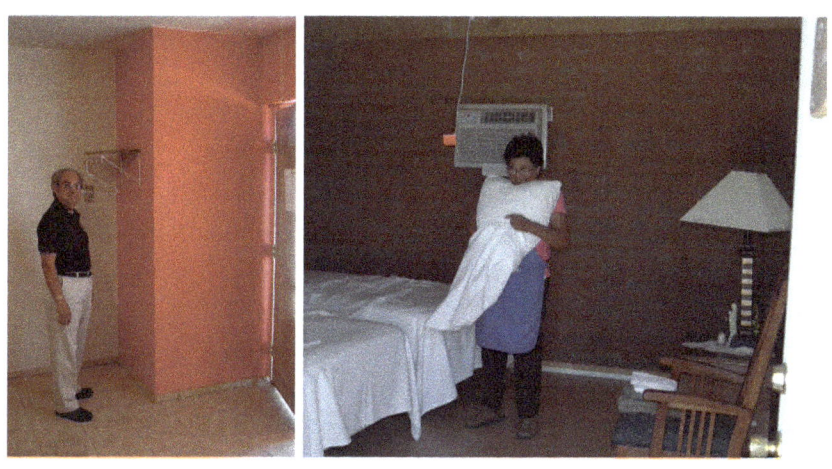

*My friends Cuco and Tencha were part
of the effort from the beginning*

I am getting a little older, my joints hurt a little bit more, but my soul is strong. When I let Holy Trinity Retreat Center go, I had no idea that this was just another one of God's plans for me. I look back at the incredible accomplishment, the toll it took on my body and how I grew as a son of God, as a Holy Man and how I am still listening to Him. He is not done with me. He has held me close to Him since I was a field worker and had dreams of a larger world. I am back to clinical medicine and am tending to the Central American Refugees throughout the El Paso area. This is living the Gospel. I am also mentoring/lecturing high school students at the Upward Bound Program at UTEP where I was a student over 45 years ago. I am also volunteering as clinical faculty for Texas Tech Foster School of Medicine where I completed my residency 37 years ago. My Camino continues and I try to listen. I am very imperfect, I have been broken many times, but the Camino is perfect and no permission is needed to embrace it, even when you fall or when you feel lost.

I injured my right knee recently, but my backpack is ready and awaits me patiently because I have another walk planned for May and as many as my Lord gives me permission to walk with Him.

Buen Camino!

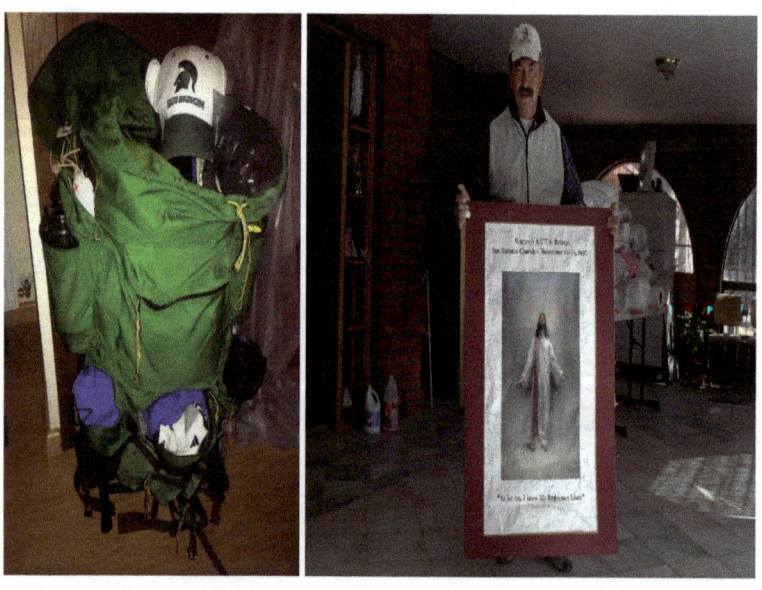

ABOUT THE AUTHOR

Ascension Mena is an Executive Physician in El Paso, Texas. He specializes in Medical Management and has practiced Emergency Medicine and Family Medicine for 35 years in El Paso. He has been Medical Director of La Fe Clinic, Bienvivir Senior Services, Life Ambulance, Ysleta Del Sur Pueblo Health Services, and the Texas Department of Ageing and Disabilities Center in El Paso. He provides care for Central American Refugees and volunteers throughout the community. He built Holy Trinity Retreat Center and recently donated the facility. He has studied the health care systems of the People's Republic of China, the Philippines, and Costa Rica. He is a Clinical Assistant Professor for the Paul Foster School of Medicine and volunteers teaching at UTEP Upward Bound. He received BS and MS degrees from UT-El Paso, an MD Degree from Michigan State University, a Master's Degree in Medical Management from UT-Dallas, Pedorthic Certification from Oklahoma State University, and a completed his medical Residency from Texas Tech School of Medicine. He and his wife, MaryLynn (Mimi), live in a small farm in El Paso's lower valley and enjoy tennis, biking, and hiking.

CPSIA information can be obtained
at www.ICGtesting.com
Printed in the USA
BVHW052249300919
559810BV00023BA/1902/P